STECK-VAUGHN
PORTRAIT OF AMERICA

Mississippi

Steck-Vaughn Company

Executive Editor	Diane Sharpe
Senior Editor	Martin S. Saiewitz
Design Manager	Pamela Heaney
Photo Editor	Margie Foster
Electronic Cover Graphics	Alan Klemp

Proof Positive/Farrowlyne Associates, Inc.
Program Editorial, Revision Development, Design, and Production

Consultant: Lawanda Turnage, Mississippi Tourism Division

Published by Raintree Steck-Vaughn Publishers, an imprint of Steck-Vaughn Company.

A Turner Educational Services, Inc. book. Based on the Portrait of America television series by R. E. (Ted) Turner.

Cover Photo: Beauvoir, the Jefferson Davis Home, by © Superstock.

Library of Congress Cataloging-in-Publication Data

Thompson, Kathleen.
   Mississippi / Kathleen Thompson.
      p.   cm. — (Portrait of America)
   "Based on the Portrait of America television series"—T.p. verso.
   "A Turner book."
   Includes index.
   ISBN 0-8114-7344-9 (library binding).—ISBN 0-8114-7449-6 (softcover)
   1. Mississippi—Juvenile literature. [1. Mississippi.]
   I. Title. II. Series: Thompson, Kathleen. Portrait of America.
F341.3.T48 1996
976.2—dc20   95-25724
                                                                        CIP
                                                                         AC

Printed and Bound in the United States of America

1 2 3 4 5 6 7 8 9 10 WZ 98 97 96 95

Acknowledgments
The publishers wish to thank the following for permission to reproduce photographs:
Pp. 7, 8 © Superstock; pp. 10, 12 Archives and Library Division, Mississippi Department of Archives and History; p. 13 Mississippi Bureau of Recreation & Parks; p. 14 Port Gibson–Clairborne County Chamber of Commerce; p. 15 Vicksburg National Military Park, National Park Service; p. 17 Archives and Library Division, Mississippi Department of Archives and History; p. 18 (top) Archives and Library Division, Mississippi Department of Archives and History, (bottom) UPI/Bettmann; p. 19 AP/Wide World Photos; pp. 20, 21, 22, 23 © Les Daniels/McComb Municiple Separate School District; p. 24 Mississippi Beach Convention & Visitors Bureau; p. 26 (both) Mississippi Department of Agriculture; p. 27 (top) © Michael Reagan, (bottom) © H. Fichner/Southern Stock; p. 28 © Libby Holley; p. 29 © W. Metzen/Southern Stock; p. 30 The Town of Mayersville; p. 31 © Libby Holley; p. 32 © Superstock; p. 34 (top) Archives and Library Division, Mississippi Department of Archives and History, (bottom) © Dakin Williams; p. 35 (top, bottom left) Archives and Library Division, Mississippi Department of Archives and History, (bottom right) © Alfred Wertheimer/RCA Records; p. 36 © Superstock; p. 37 Natchez Trace Parkway, National Park Service; p. 38 © Judy Peiser/Center for Southern Folklore; p. 39 © Johnny Buzzerio/Center for Southern Folklore; p. 41 © Les Riess/Southern Stock; p. 42 Tennessee–Tombigbee Waterway Development Authority; p. 44 © A. Jenny/Southern Stock; p. 46 One Mile Up; p. 47 (left) One Mile Up, (center, right) Mississippi Tourism Division.

STECK-VAUGHN

PORTRAIT OF AMERICA

Mississippi

Kathleen Thompson

A Turner Book

RSVP

RAINTREE
STECK-VAUGHN
PUBLISHERS

The Steck-Vaughn Company

Austin, Texas

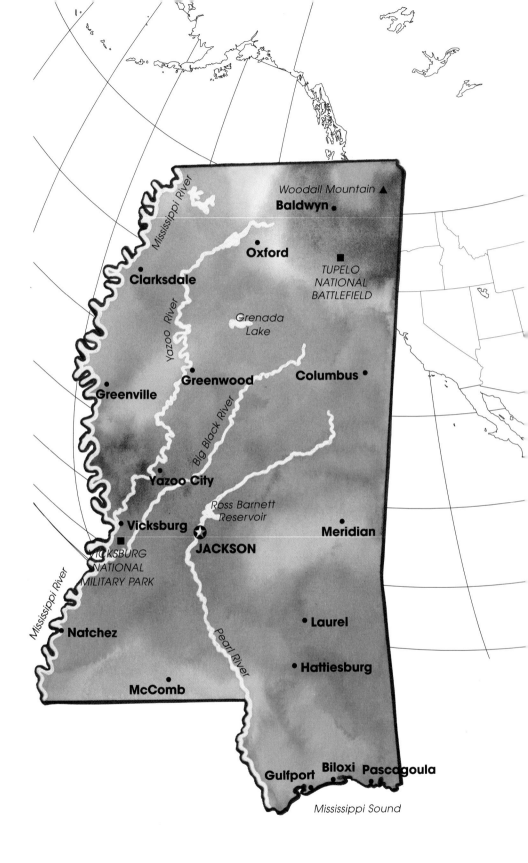

Mississippi

Woodall Mountain ▲

Baldwyn

Oxford

TUPELO
NATIONAL
BATTLEFIELD

Clarksdale

Mississippi River

Yazoo River

Grenada
Lake

Greenwood

Columbus

Greenville

Big Black River

Yazoo City

Ross Barnett
Reservoir

Vicksburg

Meridian

VICKSBURG
NATIONAL
MILITARY PARK

JACKSON

Mississippi River

Laurel

Natchez

Pearl River

Hattiesburg

McComb

Gulfport   Biloxi Pascagoula

Mississippi Sound

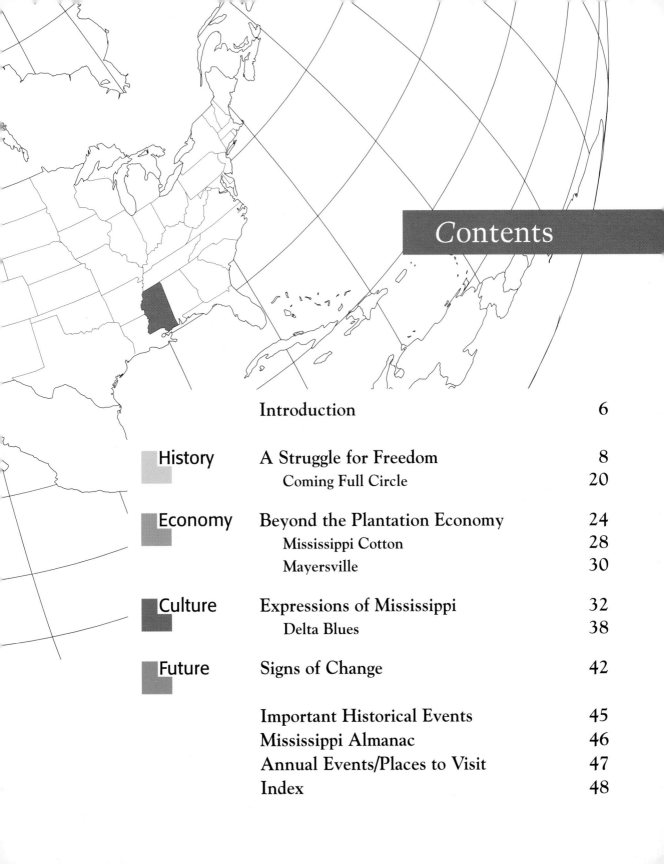

Contents

Introduction   6

History   A Struggle for Freedom   8
     Coming Full Circle   20

Economy   Beyond the Plantation Economy   24
     Mississippi Cotton   28
     Mayersville   30

Culture   Expressions of Mississippi   32
     Delta Blues   38

Future   Signs of Change   42

Important Historical Events   45
Mississippi Almanac   46
Annual Events/Places to Visit   47
Index   48

Introduction

Early Native Americans called Mississippi "the land of great waters." The powerful Mississippi River forms the state's western border. Thousands of years of flooding have left the soil along the river dark and rich. Five more large rivers cross the western and central regions of the state, emptying into the Mississippi River. Three large rivers cross the eastern part of the state. They run into the Gulf of Mexico, which forms Mississippi's southern border. This bounty of water makes Mississippi beautifully green. It is a state teeming with life, an ideal place for farming, fishing, shipping, and logging.

While riverboats remind us of Mississippi's past, they are still used to transport passengers, cargo, and vehicles.

Mississippi

$\mathcal{A}$ Struggle for Freedom

About five hundred years ago, three groups of Native Americans lived in present-day Mississippi. The Natchez lived in the southwestern region, along the Mississippi River. The Natchez were farmers who had a highly developed religion based on sun worship. Their society was divided into class systems of nobility and common people. The northeastern region was the home of the Chickasaw. The Choctaw, the largest of the three groups, lived in the south-central area. The Choctaw and the Chickasaw had much in common. Both of these groups were farming peoples who also hunted and fished. They also spoke similar languages.

The Spanish explorer Hernando de Soto was the first European to enter the area. In 1540 he led a group of soldiers west from Florida on a search for gold. They spent the winter camped by the Pontotoc River in northeastern Mississippi. In 1541 de Soto and his group continued west until they reached the Mississippi River. Then they followed the river south to the Gulf of Mexico.

Jefferson Davis, the President of the Confederacy during the Civil War, spent his last years at Beauvoir, his home in Biloxi.

In 1682 a French explorer named René-Robert Cavelier, Sieur de La Salle, led a crew down the Mississippi River from its source near the Great Lakes to the Gulf of Mexico. Realizing the great importance of this mighty waterway, La Salle claimed the entire Mississippi Valley for France.

French settlers began arriving in present-day Mississippi following La Salle's claim. Then, in 1698 English traders also arrived and began bartering with the Chickasaw for furs. This upset the French, who wanted the fur trade to themselves. In 1699 the French, led by Pierre LeMoyne, Sieur d'Iberville, built Fort Maurepas to protect their territory from the English. The fort was built on the shore of the Gulf of Mexico, just east of where Biloxi is now. Seventeen years later the French built Fort Rosalie on the Mississippi River at the site of modern-day Natchez.

In 1729 the French governor of Fort Rosalie decided to turn the land surrounding the fort into farmland. This land and the fort itself, however, were in the middle of land already occupied by the Natchez. The French governor ordered the Native Americans to

Fort Rosalie in Natchez was built by the French in 1716. It was the first fort on the Mississippi River.

move. This made the Natchez so angry that they attacked Fort Rosalie and other French settlements along the Mississippi River. French soldiers fought back. By 1731 the French had wiped out the Natchez.

In 1754 the French and the British began fighting over colonial territory along the East Coast. This conflict was called the French and Indian War. The Choctaw sided with the French, and the Chickasaw fought alongside the British. France lost the war and in 1763 signed a treaty giving Great Britain all the French land east of the Mississippi River.

Many more settlers came into the Mississippi area and began clearing forests to make farms. Then, in 1775 the original 13 colonies declared their independence from Great Britain. The Americans won the Revolutionary War in 1783 and formed the new nation of the United States. In 1798 the United States Congress created the Mississippi Territory. The area included about half the land that is now the state of Mississippi. It also included much of what would later become Alabama.

In 1803 the United States made a deal with France that became known as the Louisiana Purchase. The United States paid $15 million for all the land from the Mississippi River to the Rocky Mountains. Traffic on the Mississippi River increased. Natchez was one of its most important ports.

On December 10, 1817, the western part of the Mississippi Territory became the state of Mississippi. It was the twentieth state in the Union. Natchez was its first state capital. Two years later the eastern part of the former Mississippi Territory became the state of Alabama. At that time Mississippi had a population of about forty thousand.

The primary crop grown in Mississippi in the early 1800s was cotton. In fact, it was the leading crop across the South from South Carolina to Louisiana. The southern climate was just right for growing cotton. There was great demand for cotton in Great Britain and in the New England states, which needed it for textile manufacturing. Also, the cotton gin increased the production of cotton. This machine could separate cotton fibers from seeds as rapidly as fifty workers could.

Between the Yazoo and Mississippi rivers, there is a wide, flat stretch of land. The area has been flooded many times when the rivers overflow their banks. Some of the mud carried by the water is left behind when the water recedes. This gives the area some of the richest, most fertile soil in the world. Geologists call this area an alluvial, or a delta. Mississippians refer to the area as "the Delta." This is where many of Mississippi's large cotton plantations were located.

The Choctaw and the Chickasaw owned two thirds of the land in Mississippi. They had been given

The Paragon Gin, a cotton gin in Canton in central Mississippi, was typical of the processing plants around the turn of the century. This photo was taken about 1904.

the land through treaties signed with the federal government. Their land was in the central and northern areas of the state. At the time the treaties were signed, after statehood, all the farming and trade in the state was in the west along the Mississippi River.

With the increasing demand for cotton, farmers wanted more land to grow it. They wanted to clear the forests in the north to plant cotton. The federal government decided to take the land away from the Native Americans so the cotton farmers could have it. The government gave the Native Americans land more than six hundred miles to the northwest in present-day Oklahoma. In 1838 the United States Army forced the Choctaw and the Chickasaw to walk to this new "Indian Territory." Many Native Americans died on the long, difficult march.

During this time in the nation's history, Americans were wrestling with the issue of slavery. While plantation owners used slaves to work the land, many other people believed that slavery was wrong. In 1832 Mississippi adopted a new state constitution, which did not allow slaves to be brought into Mississippi. Even so, the number of slaves continued to grow because the children of slaves were considered to be slaves.

By 1860 more than half of Mississippi's 790,000 people were slaves. About 31,000 people owned slaves, but only about 317 of these owned more than 100 slaves. These were the large plantation owners who

Twenty-two buildings at Florewood River Plantation in Greenwood were restored to show what life was like on a cotton plantation before the Civil War.

The Rosswood Plantation in Lorman in southwestern Mississippi was built in 1857.

became wealthy from cotton. They built large homes and furnished them with the finest goods from Europe. Because of their wealth, they had great influence over Mississippi's lawmakers. They wanted to protect their comfortable way of life.

But their way of life would soon end. In 1861 Abraham Lincoln was elected President of the United States. The many differences between the North and the South over the issues of slavery, states' rights, and economics became more and more obvious. In 1861 seven states, all of them from the South, withdrew from the Union. Mississippi was the second state to do so. These states made up the Confederate States of America. Soon after, four other states from the South joined the Confederate states. President Lincoln tried to persuade the Southern states to rejoin the Union, but all efforts failed. The Civil War had begun.

During the war about eighty thousand soldiers from Mississippi fought for the Confederacy. At the same time, thousands of slaves escaped to fight for the North. More than five hundred battles were fought in Mississippi during the war. Many of them were minor skirmishes. One Mississippi battle, however, turned the tide of the war. That was the Battle of Vicksburg.

The Confederacy had won most of the battles before May 1863. Its army was largely supplied by boats sailing north on the Mississippi River. The Union leaders knew that gaining control of the river would be an enormous advantage because they could stop the flow of supplies to Southern states along the river. If the Union controlled the river, it would also divide the South in two. The Mississippi River was defended by a Confederate fort at Vicksburg, about eighty miles north of Natchez. General Ulysses S. Grant and the Union Army attacked Vicksburg in May 1863. For 47 days cannons from warships on the river and on land bombarded the town. The Confederate Army at Vicksburg finally surrendered on July 4, 1863. The Mississippi River belonged to the Union.

The Confederacy surrendered to the Union in 1865. The South had suffered greatly during the war. Much

The Battle of Vicksburg was a turning point in the Civil War. Not only did the victory give the Union control of the Mississippi River, it also provided Union troops with much-needed confidence.

work needed to be done to rebuild it and to reunite the country. The ten-year period following the war is called Reconstruction. Among the government's goals was to guarantee the rights of freed slaves. The government wanted to bring them into the political and economic life of the South.

The majority of citizens in Mississippi agreed to support the Thirteenth Amendment to the United States Constitution, outlawing slavery. But they soon passed a series of laws called the "Black Codes." These laws robbed African Americans of most of their rights as citizens, such as owning land and running for government office. Then, in 1867 Mississippi refused to accept the Fourteenth Amendment, which guaranteed the right to vote to all adult males, regardless of race. At this point, the federal government stepped in and placed Mississippi under military rule. A new constitutional convention was called. The new constitution guaranteed the vote to all adult males and provided free education for all. Mississippi was allowed back into the Union on February 23, 1870.

A newly organized Republican party took political control of the state. A number of African Americans were elected to important state offices, including lieutenant governor, senator, and legislator. Many Mississippians violently opposed the new government, however. They did not want African Americans to have any political power at all. Some joined secret organizations, such as the Ku Klux Klan. African Americans were attacked by members of the Klan, and many African Americans were killed.

In 1875 the Democratic party gained a majority in the state legislature. At that time, the Democrats were opposed to African Americans becoming a part of a free society. They forced the governor to resign and impeached the African American lieutenant governor. In 1890 the Democrats created a new state constitution that took away the voting rights given in the 1870 state constitution. African Americans were once again shut out of the government.

Mississippi was also suffering economic trouble. The war had ruined many farms and towns in Mississippi and throughout the South. The once wealthy state of Mississippi became one of the poorest in the country.

Freed slaves and other poor farmers worked as tenant farmers or sharecroppers. That meant they farmed land that belonged to someone else and handed

Living conditions were desperately poor in Mississippi during the Great Depression, especially for African American sharecroppers.

Major floods swamped the Mississippi Delta region in 1927. About one hundred thousand people had to flee their flooded homes. The total damage was more than two hundred million dollars.

This photo shows a freedom rider being arrested and searched in Jackson. During the civil rights movement, freedom riders of all races rode buses to protest against segregation.

over a large share of their crops to the owner. Most sharecroppers were constantly in debt to the landowners for supplies. Mississippi had found itself in a terrible cycle of poverty. The state had depended on agriculture for so long, there was hardly any other industry. Many people continued to farm because they could find no other way to make a living.

In 1927 floods hit the Delta area, leaving a hundred thousand people without homes. The Great Depression of the 1930s brought more hard times. Many businesses suffered financial collapses. Millions of people were unemployed, and banks and businesses across the country closed.

In 1936 Mississippi established the "Balance Agriculture with Industry" program to break the state's dependence on farming. It set up plans to attract new businesses to Mississippi by giving companies tax breaks and other advantages.

Mississippi's economy improved when the United States became involved in World War II in 1941. Its factories made supplies for the war effort. After the war the state's economy continued to grow.

The federal government was at the core of further change in 1954. In that year the United States Supreme Court ruled that segregation was unconstitutional. African Americans in Mississippi and other southern states were segregated, or separated, from others in public schools, restaurants, and other facilities. It wasn't until eight years later, however, that the first African American student was allowed into a desegregated public school in Mississippi.

In 1962 James Meredith, an African American, sought admission to the University of Mississippi. The night before he was to attend his first classes, a mob attacked the National Guard troops that had been sent to protect him. The riot claimed two lives, and 375 people were injured. However, James Meredith was admitted to the university, and he graduated.

By the 1970s manufacturing had replaced agriculture as Mississippi's main source of income. By 1990 nearly one fourth of Mississippi's population was employed in manufacturing. High-tech industries in aerospace and engineering have also recently found a home in Mississippi. Armed with an improved economy and holding on to its most treasured traditions, Mississippi is eager to take on the challenges the new century will bring.

In 1962 James Meredith became the first African American student to attend the University of Mississippi.

Coming Full Circle

When Les Daniels thinks back to the early 1960s in McComb, Mississippi, he remembers a time of suffering, anger, and terror. African American residents demanded equality. They wanted to vote in elections. They wanted their children to attend school with the other children. They insisted that things had to change. But when change came to McComb, it ripped the town apart.

Les Daniels recalls the day he learned about the trouble in his hometown of McComb. He was stationed in Germany in 1962. One Sunday morning his roommate came rushing into the room with a newspaper. "He rushed in and he said, 'Man, you better go home. They're bombing your hometown McComb.'" Some people in racially divided McComb had thrown firebombs at businesses that were owned by African Americans.

What had happened in McComb was not unusual in the South in the 1960s. African Americans were just beginning to get involved in the political process again after many years.

Les Daniels was a soldier stationed in Germany when he heard that violence and firebombings had broken out in his Mississippi hometown.

They wanted to change the system that treated them unfairly. In 1962 African Americans in McComb were going into town in great numbers to register to vote, and the people of McComb resisted. Some people who were opposed to the registration drive took action by burning the property of African Americans who registered.

20

Today, things are different in McComb. When Les Daniels came back from Germany, he got a job teaching. Then he became principal of McComb High School. While he held that post, Daniels saw to it that the school included students and teachers of all races. McComb High School also won a National Model School award. McComb was the only school from Mississippi, and also one of the smallest, to win the award that year. Not only that, but Daniels was the only African American high school principal invited to receive an award at the ceremony. Daniels remembers how it felt to be one of the guests of honor.

"It was heartwarming to be among high schools from the larger cities, from some of the larger and wealthier states. . . . I can see changes that are taking place in our students' lives. And I can say to myself, 'Hey, you had something to do with the history of this state.'"

In January 1989, Daniels took yet another history-making step. He was the first African American to be

For eleven years, Les Daniels served as principal of McComb's integrated high school. Today he is the town's superintendent of schools.

In 1983 Principal Les Daniels won a National Model School award for providing educational excellence.

appointed superintendent of the McComb School District. In 1994 Daniels received the Golden Lamp Award. This is the highest award a school administrator can attain.

While working as superintendent, Daniels also earned a doctorate in educational administration from the University of Southern Mississippi. Daniels is not satisfied with what he has accomplished so far. His current goal is to improve his students' reading scores. Currently the student population in McComb is about sixty percent African American. The teachers in the district are about forty percent African American. Daniels admits that there still is a race-relations problem in the McComb community. However, he is proud that his school district has not missed one day because of racial incidents. Daniels also does not feel an educator's job is to correct social ills. "As a professional educator, I'd like to spend my time doing what I've been trained to do," he says. "If I could do that, and not have to worry about social problems, our reading, writing, and math scores would improve."

Despite the progress in McComb, Daniels knows there's a long way to go. He feels that race relations in his hometown actually were better ten years ago than today. "I think the economic ills of the country are partly to blame. When the economy is good, race relations are not a problem."

Daniels says the students in McComb's schools have no problems being together. "The kids get along just fine. When adults get involved, however, prejudice becomes prominent. I wish the adults would listen to their children. They could learn a great deal just by watching how the students are able to get along."

Les Daniels received his doctorate degree from the University of Southern Mississippi in 1990.

Beyond the Plantation Economy

It has been nearly a century and a half since cotton made Mississippi plantation owners rich. Their way of life—and the economy it was based on—ended with the Civil War. But cotton remained the state's main crop until well into this century. Today it is just one of a wide variety of products that make up an increasingly healthy economy.

Nearly two thirds of Mississippi's annual income is obtained from service industries. In service industries, workers serve other people instead of making an actual product. The two largest parts of Mississippi's service industry are wholesale and retail trade. Wholesale trade is selling products to a business, usually in large quantities. Retail trade is selling items to an individual buyer. Other service industries in Mississippi include the state government, banking, insurance, and real estate. Jackson, the state capital and largest city, is one of the leading financial centers in the South.

Manufacturing provides more than a quarter of the income made by the state each year. The leading

Shrimp fishing is important to Mississippi's economy.

above. Today, cotton picking machines have replaced the backbreaking picking by hand of earlier times.

below. Soybeans have replaced cotton as Mississippi's main crop.

manufacturing activity is food processing, which includes canning and packaging. The next largest area of manufacturing, in terms of income, is transportation equipment, especially shipbuilding. Pascagoula, on the Gulf Coast, is one of the nation's leading shipyards. During World War II, it built both cargo ships and warships. Today it concentrates on huge tankers and freighters.

Companies in Mississippi also manufacture electrical machinery and equipment. Factories in Mississippi produce stereo systems, telephones, lighting products, household appliances, and industrial generators and motors. Wood products, such as paper and furniture, are also an important part of the state's economy. Slightly more than half the state is covered with forests, so Mississippi is also one of the nation's leading lumber producers.

Even though manufacturing passed farming as the state's largest source of income in 1965, agriculture still makes an important contribution. Mississippi's major agricultural products are soybeans, cotton, poultry, cattle, rice, wheat, and sweet potatoes. Peaches, watermelons, and grapes are the leading fruits, and pecans and greenhouse and nursery plants also flourish. Because of its warm climate, fertile land, and abundant water, Mississippi is a good place to farm.

Fishing is also a significant source of income for the state. Buffalo fish, carp, and catfish are caught in the state's many rivers. Fishing boats in the Gulf of Mexico catch red snapper, a popular food fish, and menhaden, which is used to make fertilizer. Oysters and shrimp are a major industry along the Gulf Coast, particularly around Biloxi. Mississippi's fastest-growing business is catfish farming. The fish are raised in huge, shallow artificial lakes. Mississippi supplies eighty percent of the farm-raised catfish consumed in the world.

Mining plays a small but significant role in the state's economy. In 1939 and 1940, oil was discovered in two locations near the center of the state. Since then more deposits have been found in the southern sections and below the shallow waters of the Gulf Coast. These deposits make Mississippi one of the nation's leading producers of petroleum. In 1963 a huge refinery was built at Pascagoula to process the state's oil.

Mississippi has good natural resources and hard-working people. In 1959 its per capita income was only 51 percent of the national average. By 1993 it was about seventy percent and still climbing. Though more progress needs to be made, Mississippi has a good start.

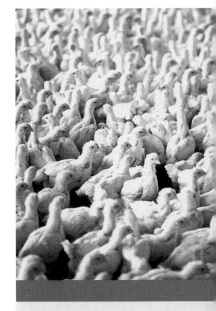

Mississippi is one of the leading chicken-producing states in the nation.

This is one of Mississippi's marinas along the Gulf of Mexico. Fishing in the Gulf of Mexico produces 16 percent of the nation's ocean fish catch.

Mississippi Cotton

The cotton plant is useful in hundreds of ways, from making adhesive tape to blue jeans to isolation suits for astronauts. Clothing made from cotton is worn by three fourths of the world's people. Is it any wonder cotton is considered one of the world's most important crops?

The United States produces more cotton than any other country except China. Mississippi produces more cotton than all the states except Texas and California. Mississippi produces over 748 million pounds of cotton a year!

Much of Mississippi's cotton is grown in the northwestern part of the state. Cotton plants grow best in a warm-to-hot climate with about 180 frost-free days. They need rich, well-drained soil that holds in water. Mississippi's Delta region, along the Mississippi River, is the perfect cotton-growing environment.

Each cotton plant grows from a seed to a seedling and then becomes a flowering plant. When the flowers

Cotton fields have been a common sight in Mississippi for nearly two centuries.

A cotton harvester pulls cotton from the boll and blows it into a large steel basket at the back of the machine.

drop off, a pod—called a boll—forms. The boll contains the cotton seeds and the cotton fibers. For about ten weeks, the cotton fibers grow and thicken as the boll ripens. Then it splits open, and the fibers begin to dry in the sun. Soon, the cotton is ready to be picked.

Picking machines pull the cotton from the boll. Each machine can do the work it used to take forty people to do by hand. Next, the cotton goes into a cotton gin, a machine that dries, cleans, and removes the cotton seeds. The seeds are used for other purposes, such as making cottonseed oil and growing more seedlings. The fibers are packed into bales and sent to markets and cotton exchanges. Each bale of cotton weighs 480 pounds and is about the size of a refrigerator. Cotton merchants buy thousands of bales of cotton for use in spinning cloth and making other products.

To prepare for the next growing season, Mississippi cotton growers plow the cotton stalks back into the soil. Then, they fertilize and irrigate their fields. Next, they buy more cotton seeds. It's a steady and profitable business. Growing cotton has been a part of Mississippi for well over a hundred years. And as long as the Mississippi River keeps soaking the rich Delta soil, there will always be cotton bolls waving in the warm Mississippi breeze.

Mayersville

Unita Blackwell, and the town she grew up in, are symbols of the new Mississippi. "My father was a sharecropper," Ms. Blackwell recalls. "That's the way I was raised up—you know, picking cotton and hoeing and trying to find a way to learn how to read and write. It's a strange feeling to go down to the river to think about that my ancestors were slaves coming through that path. . . . "

The world Unita Blackwell was born into has changed. This sharecropper's daughter became the first African American woman mayor in Mississippi. When she was a little girl, that would not have been thought possible. Her town, Mayersville, has only a few hundred people, but they are working together. One reason they are is that Unita Blackwell is a woman of vision. What she brought to the mayor's office was not only her own vision, but also insight from the other side of the world.

"I left this country in 1973 and I went to China. I saw a whole different world. It gave me a different perspective on life. I realized that I wasn't the only person who had suffered. I saw that African Americans in America were not the only people who had to struggle. It makes a difference when you understand that."

With this new insight, Unita Blackwell came back to her town. The small community near the Mississippi River wasn't even incorporated. This meant that it could not receive many kinds of grants from the federal government. Ms. Blackwell started working, a

The mayor's office in the Mayersville town hall seems a long way from the sharecropper's shack where Unita Blackwell grew up.

Unita Blackwell was the first African American woman to serve as a town mayor in Mississippi.

little at a time, to make things better for her friends and neighbors. But more importantly, she inspired them to work for themselves. She ran for mayor in 1976 and won. In that same year, Mayersville became incorporated.

Along with incorporation came new challenges. She received fifty thousand dollars from the federal government for a fire truck—the first in the town's history. She also received two hundred thousand dollars for public housing for the elderly and disabled, but she was not able to buy the necessary land. For ten years she tried to find land for this project, and in 1986 she succeeded. It is one of her proudest accomplishments.

Another accomplishment was a town sewer system. "We never had a sewer system. Now we do, and it's ours. But we're going to have to maintain it. If we don't, who will?" Mayor Blackwell brought that attitude of "we can do it" to the town of Mayersville.

Unita Blackwell did not seek re-election in 1993. She wanted to take time off from politics. However, in 1995 she was elected to the town council. She feels she still has much to offer her town.

Expressions of Mississippi

Writers and musicians are an important part of the culture of any state. They bring to our eyes and ears the beauty, the pain, and the powerful emotions of life in a certain time and place. Many talented Mississippi writers and musicians have shared their visions with the rest of the world.

Some say William Faulkner was the greatest writer ever to come out of the South. In his novels he created an imaginary world set in rural Mississippi. Faulkner's books are full of darkness, love, and humor. He wrote about common human traits and contrasted them with universal values, such as love, honor, and compassion. In 1949 William Faulkner won the Nobel Prize for literature. In 1955 he won the Pulitzer Prize for *A Fable*, a story about a World War I soldier. In 1963 he won another Pulitzer for *The Reivers*, which tells of the humorous adventures of a boy who takes a trip from Mississippi to Tennessee.

William Faulkner spent most of his life in Oxford in north-central Mississippi. The graceful mansion that

Natchez, the oldest town on the Mississippi River, hosts an annual tour of its antebellum, or pre-Civil War, homes. This photo is of Dunleith, which was built in 1856.

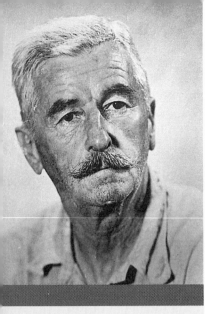

William Faulkner worked for a time as a scriptwriter in Hollywood.

"Tennessee" is a name Williams used professionally. His real name was Thomas Lanier Williams.

he called home was built in 1848. It has been restored and is now a popular tourist attraction.

Tennessee Williams was another Mississippi writer who was twice awarded the Pulitzer Prize. Williams is best known as a playwright, although he also wrote poetry and fiction. He won his first Pulitzer Prize in 1948 for his play *A Streetcar Named Desire*. He won his second in 1955 for *Cat on a Hot Tin Roof*.

Eudora Welty was born in Jackson, Mississippi, in 1909 and has lived in the state her entire life. Welty, known mainly for her short stories and novels, won the Pulitzer Prize in 1973 for *The Optimist's Daughter*. In her books she portrays small-town southern life with a sharp wit and warm sensitivity.

Richard Wright was a Mississippi writer who was one of the first major novelists to write about the African American experience. His novel *Native Son* is a powerful portrayal of racism in America. Among Wright's other notable works are *Black Boy*, his personal story of growing up near Natchez, and *Uncle Tom's Children*, a collection of short stories set in the racially divided Mississippi of his childhood.

Mississippi has also produced many very different musicians from every part of the musical spectrum. For example, Elvis Presley, the "King of Rock 'n' Roll," grew up and had his musical roots in rural Mississippi. By contrast, Leontyne Price is a Mississippi opera singer who has enchanted audiences worldwide. Price was the first African American woman to sing at La Scala in Milan, Italy. William Grant Still, a composer and conductor, was the first African American to conduct an American symphony orchestra. Charley Pride is the first famous African American performer of country music. Another country music singer from Mississippi is Tammy Wynette. She was named female vocalist of the year by the Country Music Association three years in a row.

Several other notable entertainers have also come from Mississippi. James Earl Jones is a distinguished African American actor. He won several Tony Awards for his work on stage and has appeared in countless movies and television shows. Talk show star Oprah Winfrey hosts one of the most popular programs on daytime television. She comes from the town of

Eudora Welty is one of Mississippi's most beloved writers.

Leontyne Price is one of the first African American international opera stars.

Rock 'n' roll superstar Elvis Presley was born and raised in Tupelo, Mississippi. This photo shows him as a young man just at the start of his fame.

This is the parlor of Jefferson Davis's home, Beauvoir. The grounds include a cemetery and a Confederate museum.

Kosciusko, which is almost in the center of the state. Finally, Jim Henson, who created the Muppets and the puppet characters on "Sesame Street," also hailed from Mississippi.

The culture of Mississippi is not limited to writers and performers. Before the Civil War, some plantation owners in Mississippi lived in elegant mansions. Many of these mansions were destroyed in the war, but some remain and have been restored. They provide a fascinating look at a bygone era. From the long verandah porches framed by white pillars to the imported European furniture, they show a way of life that is gone forever.

Some of the loveliest examples are in the city of Natchez. One of these homes, named Longwood, has an ornate central-domed tower. Another notable home, called Rosalie, was built in a less ornate but still elegant style. Melrose is one of the loveliest of the Natchez homes. It's set like a jewel in the center of lush gardens. Other Mississippi towns with historic homes include Vicksburg and Columbus.

Civil War battles raged throughout Mississippi for four years, and many of these battlefields have been restored as memorials. Vicksburg, the site of one of the most important battles of the war, has the Vicksburg National Military Park. It contains the trenches, gun emplacements, and rifle pits used by the Confederate defenders.

Another Civil War memorial is Brices Cross Roads National Battlefield, near Baldwyn, in north-eastern Mississippi. It marks the site where 3,500

Confederate troops won a victory over 8,000 Union soldiers. Less than twenty miles south of this site is the Tupelo National Battlefield. Here the Union won one of the last Civil War battles fought in Mississippi.

Another way to sample the culture of Mississippi is to visit some of its fine museums. The Delta Blues Museum in Clarksdale traces the history of Mississippi music. Both Jackson and Laurel have notable art museums. Jackson also is home to the Mississippi Museum of Natural Science and the Mississippi State Historical Museum.

Mississippi is a state with a rich heritage and a colorful history. Add to that its lush, green surroundings, and Mississippi just naturally lends itself to expression. Like gifts on a table, the people of Mississippi want to add something of their own to an already beautiful and bountiful state.

There are two cannons and two monuments at the Civil War battlefield in Tupelo. They are dedicated to the memory of the soldiers who fought there.

Delta Blues

There is a very special sound that comes from the Mississippi Delta. It is not as old as the sound of farming or of songbirds. However, in some ways it is as old as time itself. It is what is known as the Delta blues.

The blues began in the 1890s. It is a combination of African American gospel church music, work songs, and dance hall music. Most blues songs talk about trouble—money trouble, marriage trouble, or trouble with the law. Such troubles make people feel "blue," or sad. Usually people play the blues for themselves and their friends.

For more than fifty years, blues singer Son Thomas played and sang about troubled lives and hard times.

John Lee Hooker was a Delta blues musician who migrated to the North. He settled in Detroit, helping to bring the blues to new audiences.

In the Mississippi Delta, the blues were usually performed by a singer with a guitar.

Son Thomas was born in 1927 in Yazoo City, on the eastern edge of the Delta. By the time he was ten years old, he was playing the blues on borrowed guitars. His first guitar was a Gene Autry model from the Sears Roebuck catalog. "It cost $8.50," he recalled. "I picked cotton to make enough money to get that guitar. Then I played on the post office steps and made my money back."

Like many of the older bluesmen, Son Thomas knew the backbreaking labor of the cotton fields. "It's hard to pick a hundred pounds of cotton from sunup to sundown. Singing the blues, late over in the evening, about quitting time—it kind of relieves your mind and makes you not worry too hard."

For poor people of any race, there is much to worry about. "The blues is a worried mind," says Reverend Rubin Lacy, a former blues singer. "It all boils down to worry."

One thing many blues singers have had to worry about is money. For every Delta blues performer who has become rich and famous, dozens have not. Most still sing on front porches and in roadside bars, doing farmwork to earn a living. Son Thomas made several albums late in his life. But they never sold enough to make him much money.

Some do make it big, of course. The number of famous blues stars who came from the Delta makes a very impressive list. There's B. B. King from Indianola and Muddy Waters from Rolling Fork. John Lee Hooker came from Clarksdale. Bo Diddley was born in McComb. In the early part of this century, Robert Johnson, from Robinsville, and "Big Bill" Broonzy, from Scott, were two of the first blues stars.

Blues music began to branch out in the 1920s when many African Americans left the Delta because of poverty and racial oppression. Many blues musicians got jobs playing in cities such as St. Louis, Memphis, and Chicago.

Sunnyland Slim was one such musician who left the Delta for a better opportunity elsewhere. He was born Albert Luandrew in Vance, Mississippi, in 1908. By the time he

was 15 years old, he was playing in various places throughout the Delta. He moved to Memphis in the late 1920s and began working with the now-famous blues musicians Little Brother Montgomery and Ma Rainey. Sunnyland Slim, who took his name from the Sunnyland, a train that traveled between Memphis and St. Louis, moved to Chicago in 1939. There he stayed, teaming up with Muddy Waters and a number of other blues musicians.

The migration of blues musicians brought this musical form to many more appreciative audiences. The blues became so well-liked, especially on Beale Street in Memphis and in Chicago's South Side, that other musical forms have grown from its influence. In the 1930s "boogie-woogie" became popular as an up-tempo, piano-based version of blues music. "Rhythm and blues" followed this path in the 1950s by adding a few more instruments, such as horns. Rock-and-roll musicians, such as British guitarist Eric Clapton, also acknowledge their musical debt to the blues.

But no matter how popular it becomes or how it is adapted or changed, the blues still has its roots in hard times in the Delta. Son Thomas recalls those times. "You wonder, how did you make it? You wonder, how did you come through with it? You think about all what have happened. No money, no home, no car to ride in, a bunch of children. Wondering how I'm going to get money to help with them, hoping I get a job here and yonder—there's a whole lot to think of.

"I want my listeners to feel how the time was long time ago. The blues is singing the way that you live and where you're trying to go."

The sun sets over the Mississippi Delta. The Delta blues is the most-often copied of all the blues traditions.

Signs of Change

A quick look at Mississippi might show a state linked to the past. Many of the national monuments are remembrances of the Civil War. Even its state flag bears the symbol of the Confederacy. But that's not the whole story of Mississippi. Its people have decided that the past will not rule their lives. Racial separation and a depressed economy were part of the state's past. But they are not part of the state's present or its future.

Beginning with the "Balance Agriculture with Industry" program in 1936, Mississippi has recognized the need to progress. This program lowered business taxes and offered other benefits to attract industry into the state. In addition, Mississippi was one of the very first states to use advertising to attract business. Oil wells have created a new source of wealth, and tourism is encouraged.

Rivers have always provided a ready-made transportation system in the western part of the state. But the northeastern part of Mississippi did not share that natural advantage. In 1985 the Tennessee-Tombigbee

The Tennessee-Tombigbee Waterway is a 234-mile-long waterway constructed to connect the southeastern United States with the Midwest. It also helps to link Mississippi's future to the nation's economy.

Waterway was opened. This system of canals and locks links the Tennessee River to the north with the Tombigbee River farther south. The waterway has brought jobs and industry to this once isolated part of Mississippi. It is another sign that the state is moving forward.

One of the state's new industries is making high-tech parts for orbital rockets and the space shuttle. These high-tech parts include the engines that transport astronauts into space. Engines are tested at the John C. Stennis Space Center. The roar of the rocket engine and the billowing smoke are proof of how far Mississippi has come.

Mississippi still is one of the nation's leaders in cotton production, but this by itself cannot sustain the state's economy into the twenty-first century. The future of Mississippi is based upon industries that can provide for the needs of a fast-paced world.

This is the courthouse in Jackson, which is Mississippi's capital and largest city. The state will continue to rely on Jackson for leadership.

Important Historical Events

1541 Spanish explorer Hernando de Soto explores the Mississippi area.

1682 René-Robert Cavelier, Sieur de La Salle, claims the entire Mississippi Valley for France and calls it the Louisiana Territory.

1763 The Treaty of Paris gives all the French land east of the Mississippi and west of Baton Rouge to Great Britain.

1798 The Mississippi Territory is created by an act of Congress.

1803 The United States buys the Louisiana Territory, which includes present-day Mississippi, from France.

1817 Mississippi becomes the twentieth state in the Union.

1822 Jackson becomes the state capital.

1830 The Treaty of Dancing Rabbit Creek cedes all Choctaw land east of the Mississippi River to the federal government.

1861 Mississippi withdraws from the Union.

1863 Union forces take Jackson. Vicksburg surrenders.

1867 Mississippi refuses to accept the Fourteenth Amendment.

1870 Mississippi is readmitted to the Union with a constitution providing free public education, the vote for African American men, and a strong legislature.

1875 Democrats regain control of state politics. They impeach the African American lieutenant governor.

1890 A new constitution is adopted that destroys most of the gains of the 1870 constitution.

1909 Boll weevils damage the cotton crop.

1936 The Balance Agriculture with Industry program is started.

1954 The United States Supreme Court rules that segregation of public schools is unconstitutional.

1962 James Meredith is admitted to the University of Mississippi. Federal troops are brought in to stop the rioting.

1965 The Voting Rights Act is passed.

1969 Hurricane Camille destroys Mississippi's Gulf Coast.

1976 Mississippi Democrats reunite to send an African American to the National Convention.

1982 The Mississippi legislature adopts the Education Reform Act.

1985 Judge Reuben Anderson becomes the first African American Supreme Court justice in Mississippi.

1988 Drought causes large parts of Mississippi to be declared disaster areas. It is the worst drought and heat wave in the state since the 1930s.

1994 Mississippi is the first of a number of states to sue the American tobacco companies. The suit asks for the repayment of millions of tax dollars that have been spent on medical treatment of smoking-related illnesses.

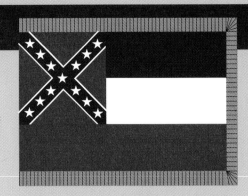

The state flag, adopted in 1894, reflects Mississippi's ties to both the United States and the Confederate States of America. The red, white, and blue stripes are the national colors of the United States. In the upper left corner is a Confederate battle flag, in which the 13 stars represent the original states of the Union.

Mississippi Almanac

Nickname. The Magnolia State

Capital. Jackson

State Bird. Mockingbird

State Flower. Magnolia

State Tree. Magnolia

State Motto. *Virtute et armis* (By valor and arms)

State Song. "Go Mis-sis-sip-pi"

State Abbreviations. Miss. (traditional); MS (postal)

Statehood. December 10, 1817, the 20th state

Government. Congress: U.S. senators, 2; U.S. representatives, 5. State Legislature: senators, 55; representatives, 122. Counties: 82

Area. 47,716 sq mi (123,584 sq km), 32nd in size among the states

Greatest Distances. north/south, 352 mi (566 km); east/west, 188 mi (303 km). Coastline: 44 mi (71 km)

Elevation. Highest: Woodall Mountain, 806 ft (246 m). Lowest: sea level, along the coast

Population. 1990 Census: 2,586,443 (3% increase over 1980), 31st among the states. Density: 54 persons per sq mi (21 persons per sq km). Distribution: 47% urban, 53% rural. 1980 Census: 2,520,631

Economy. *Agriculture:* cattle, soybeans, cotton, poultry, hogs and pigs, rice, milk, eggs. *Fishing:* catfish, shrimp. *Manufacturing:* food products, transportation equipment, electric and electronic equipment, wood products, chemicals, clothing, furniture. *Mining:* petroleum, natural gas, sand, gravel, crushed stone

State Seal

State Bird: Mockingbird

State Flower: Magnolia

Annual Events

★ Dixie National Livestock Show and Rodeo in Jackson (February)

★ Spring Pilgrimage in Natchez (March/April)

★ Mississippi Arts Festival in Jackson (April)

★ Choctaw Indian Fair in Philadelphia (July)

★ Mississippi Deep Sea Fishing Rodeo in Gulfport (July)

★ Watermelon Festival in Mize (July)

★ Delta Blues Festival in Greenville (September)

★ Seafood Festival in Biloxi (September)

★ Sky Parade in Jackson (September)

★ The Great Mississippi River Balloon Race (October)

★ Mississippi State Fair in Jackson (October)

Places to Visit

★ Biloxi Lighthouse, built in 1848

★ Brices Cross Roads National Battlefield Site, near Baldwyn

★ Capitol building in Jackson

★ Delta Blues Museum in Clarksdale

★ Fort Massachusetts, on Ship Island

★ Grand Gulf Military Monument Park in Port Gibson

★ Natchez National Historical Park in Natchez

★ Petrified Forest, near Flora

★ Rosemont Plantation, boyhood home of Jefferson Davis, in Woodville

★ State Historical Museum in Jackson

★ Tupelo National Battlefield, near Tupelo

★ Vicksburg National Military Park, near Vicksburg

★ William Faulkner's home in Oxford

Index

African Americans, 30–31, 34, 35, 38, 40
   discrimination against, 16–18, 19, 20–23
agriculture, 12, 13, 18, 19, 26, 43
Battle of Vicksburg, 15
Black Codes, 16
blues, 38–41
Brices Cross Roads National Battlefield, 36–37
Broonzy, "Big Bill," 40
Chickasaw, 9, 10, 11, 12–13
Choctaw, 9, 11, 12–13
Civil War, 9, 15, 36–37, 43
commercial fishing, 25, 26–27
Confederacy, 9, 14–15, 36–37, 43
cotton, 12–13, 14, 25, 28–29, 44
Daniels, Les, 20–23
Davis, Jefferson, 9, 36
Democratic party, 17
De Soto, Hernando, 9
Diddley, Bo, 40
education, 16, 20–23
Faulkner, William, 33–34
Florewood River Plantation, 13
Fort Maurepas, 10
Fort Rosalie, 10, 11
France, 10–11
French and Indian War, 11
fur trade, 10
Grant, Ulysses S., 15
Great Britain, 10, 11, 12
Great Depression, 17, 18
Gulf of Mexico, 6, 9, 10
Henson, Jim, 36
high-tech industry, 19, 44
Hooker, John Lee, 39, 40

Iberville, Sieur d', 10
Indian Territory, 13
industry, 18, 43
John C. Stennis Space Center, 44
Johnson, Robert, 40
Jones, James Earl, 35
King, B. B., 40
Ku Klux Klan, 16
La Salle, Sieur de, 10
Lincoln, Abraham, 14, 15
Louisiana Purchase, 11
lumber industry, 26
manufacturing, 12, 19, 25–26
Mayersville, 30–31
McComb, 20–23
Meredith, James, 19
mining, 27
Mississippi Delta, 12, 28, 38–41
Mississippi River, 6, 9, 10, 11, 12, 15
Mississippi Territory, 11, 12
Montgomery, Little Brother, 40
museums, 37
Natchez, 10, 11, 33, 36
Natchez, culture, 9, 10–11
Native Americans, 6, 9, 10–11, 12–13
oil industry, 27
Paragon Gin, 12
Pascagoula, 26, 27
plantations, 12, 13, 25, 36
Pontotoc River, 9
population, 12, 13–14, 19
Presley, Elvis, 34, 35
Price, Leontyne, 34, 35
Pride, Charley, 35

Rainey, Ma, 40
Reconstruction, 16–18
Republican party, 16
Revolutionary War, 11
Rosswood Plantation, 14
segregation, 19
service industries, 25
settlers, 10, 11
sharecroppers, 17–18, 30
slavery, 13–14, 15, 16, 30
Spain, 9
statehood, 11–12
Still, William Grant, 34–35
Sunnyland Slim, 40
Tennessee River, 44
Tennessee-Tombigbee Waterway, 43–44
Thomas, Son, 38, 39, 40, 41
Tombigbee River, 44
transportation, 43
Tupelo National Battlefield, 37
United States Constitution, 16
   Fourteenth Amendment, 16
   Thirteenth Amendment, 16
University of Mississippi, 19
Vicksburg, 15, 36
Vicksburg National Military Park, 36
Waters, Muddy, 40
Welty, Eudora, 34, 35
Williams, Tennessee, 34
Winfrey, Oprah, 35–36
World War II, 19, 26
Wright, Richard, 34
Wynette, Tammy, 35
Yazoo River, 12